Mock Paper Overview

Instructions

1. Each test needs to be completed in 35 minutes.

2. The total number of questions (including sub-questions) range from 40-50 for each test.

3. Students should ideally begin with Mock Test 1 to ensure they move from a relatively easier to difficult stage with Mock Test 5.

4. An answer key has been provided.

5. Please share a scanned version or a high-quality image of a completed mock test for a free assessment. Please email it to littlechampsltd@gmail.com with the subject "Free Assessment" and mention the name of the current school and the schools you intend to apply to.

©Little Champs Ltd

Mock Paper 1

Instructions

1. You have 35 minutes to answer the questions. Total marks 60

2. If you are unable to answer any questions, please move on to the next question

3. This is an advanced level 1 test

Solve the following

1. 25+15= _____ [1

2. 19+20= _____ [1

3. 50-15= _____ [1

4. 10 ÷ 2= _____ [1

5. 40+55= _____ [1

6. 18 x 5 = _____ [1

7. $10 \times 0 =$ _____ [1]

8. $5 \times 4 =$ _____ [1]

Answer whether each statement is True or False

9. A rectangle has same number of sides as a square _____ [1]

10. A triangle is formed of 5 sides _____ [1]

11. A hexagon has less sides than a pentagon _____ [1]

12. A circle has no vertices _____ [1]

13. Arrange the following numbers from smallest to largest. 232, 323, 189, 198, 423, 190

_____ [1]

14. Arrange the following numbers from largest to smallest. 435, 243, 463, 143, 43

_____ [1]

15. If I have five apples, four oranges and 12 bananas,

(a) how many total pieces of fruit do I have? _____

(b) how many bananas will 4 children get if the bananas are shared equally between them?

_____

(c) how many apples will be left over if I give each of the 4 children equal apples?

_____

(d) how many pieces of fruit are left to be distributed if 12 bananas and 4 apples are given away?

_____

[

Write the following numbers as words

16. 43   _____   [

17. 125   _____   [

18. 10   _____   [

19. 19   _____   [

20. 28   _____   [

21. Shade half of the image

[1]

22. Shade two thirds of the image

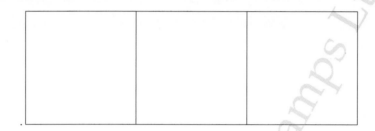

[1]

23. shade one fourth of the image

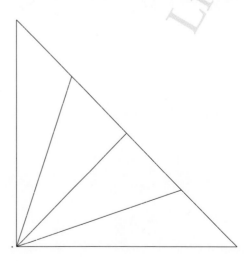

[1]

24. How many 10s make 80?   _____   [2

25. How many days does December have?   _____   [1

26. Xavier catches 5 fishes, Andrea 4 fishes and Rumi 7 fishes; how many fish have been caught?

    _____   [1

27. There are 25 flowers. Out of these, there are 12 red flowers. How many flowers aren't red?   _____   [1

28. Which is more, 45 minutes or two quarters of an hour?   _____   [2

29. If you live 45 minutes to school, quarter of an hour from the park and three quarters of an hour from the cinema

    Circle the correct answer.

    (a) What is the closest to your home, School, Park or Cinema?

    (b) The school and cinema are both similar distances from your home. True/False

    [4

30. If 3 balls cost £9, how much do 6 balls cost?   _____   [2

31. If I run 5 km in 20 mins, how much time will I run in 1 hour? ＿＿＿＿＿＿＿＿ [2]

Write the value of 4 in words

32. 450 ＿＿＿＿＿＿＿＿＿＿＿＿＿＿＿＿＿＿ [1]

33. 140 ＿＿＿＿＿＿＿＿＿＿＿＿＿＿＿＿＿＿ [1]

34. 843 ＿＿＿＿＿＿＿＿＿＿＿＿＿＿＿＿＿＿ [1]

35. 784 ＿＿＿＿＿＿＿＿＿＿＿＿＿＿＿＿＿＿ [1]

36. Fill in the squares so that the sums are correct on the right side (columns) and the bottom (rows)?

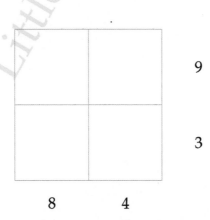

[4]

37. Draw a mirror image of the below pattern

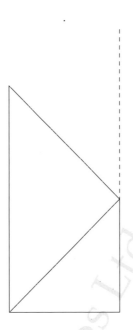

[3

Use the correct operator ($<$, $>$, $=$) to fill in the boxes

38. 20 ☐ 15

[

39. 35 ☐ 34

[1

40. 45 ☐ 56

[1

41. $\frac{1}{4}$ ☐ $\frac{2}{4}$

[

42. $\frac{5}{10}$ ☐ $\frac{2}{4}$

[

43. Rounding of 18 to the nearest ten gives us _____ [1]

44. Write the time 10:15 am in words _____ [1]

45. Write the time in words? _____ [1]

End of Mock Test. Please hand over the paper for assessment.

Mock Paper 2

Instructions

1. You have 35 minutes to answer the questions. Total marks 53

2. If you are unable to answer any questions, please move on to the next question

3. This is an advanced level 2 test

---

1. I have a big cake and give away 1/5th each to Rory and Symlie, 2/5th to Zoe, and the rest to Dora.

(a) Who gets the largest share of the cake? _____

(b) How much cake does Dora get? _____

(c) Rory and Symlie have more cake than Dora?(True/False) _____

[3

Complete the pattern; questions 2-6

2. 18   27   _____   45   [1]

3. 0   2   4   6   8   _____   12   14   16   [1]

4. $\dfrac{1}{3}$ $\dfrac{1}{6}$ _____   _____ $\dfrac{1}{15}$ $\dfrac{1}{18}$ [1]

5. 1   3   5   7   _____   _____   13   [1]

6. _____   20   30   40   _____   60   70   80   [1]

Solve questions 7-11

7. 20 + 56 = 30 + ?   _____   [1]

8. 9 x 12 =   _____   [1]

9. 20 x 5 =   _____   [1]

10. 4 x 6 = 12 + ?   _____   [1]

11. $18 \div 3 =$ _____   [

12. Jemma reads for 7 hours every week. How many hours does she read daily if she reads for the same time each day? _____   [

13. A train has left London to go to Edinburgh at 12:05 pm. It reaches its first stop after one hour and twenty-five minutes. It reaches Edinburgh at 18:35.

    (a) At what time did it reach the first stop? _____

    (b) What was the total time taken to reach Edinburgh? _____

    (c) At what time should the train leave London if it is to reach Edinburgh at 18:15? _____

                                                                                                [

    Write the following numbers as words

14. 67 _____   [

15. 485 _____ [1]

16. 035 _____ [1]

17. 59 _____ [1]

18. Complete drawing the star

[2]

Name the shapes

19. ☐ _____ [1]

20.  _____ [1

21. _____ [1

22. _____ [1

23. _____ [1

Fill in the right operator (+, -, ÷, x) or the number as required.

24. $47 + \boxed{} = 54$ [1

25. $\boxed{} - 17 = 89$ [1

26. 15 ☐ 5 = 75 [1]

27. 35 ☐ 7 = 5 [1]

28. 220 + ☐ = 240 [1]

29. 95 − ☐ = 36 [1]

Write the time in words

30. _____ [1]

31. _____ [1]

32. 15:36 _____ [1]

33. 9:40 am _____   [

34. Use a ruler to measure the below line. The line measures ____ cm.

_____

[

35. Write the value of the circled digit in the number 4 ⑤ 8

_____   [

36. Write the value of the circled digit in the number ⑧ 3 0

_____   [

37. How many centimetres equal 1 meter? _____   [

38. The total number of days in January and April is _____ days   [

39. If I left the house at 8 am and walked for 10 minutes to my friend's house and then took 25 minutes to reach school, what time did I get to school?

_____   [

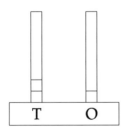

Example of the abacus with 2 tens beads and 1 ones bead

40. For an abacus showing tens and ones, answer the following questions.

   (a) What is the smallest two-digit number you can make with three beads?

   _____

   (b) How many different 2 digit numbers can you make with two beads?

   _____

[3]

41. Arrange the following numbers from smallest to largest: 34 235 23 56 32 24 19

   _____   [1]

42. Arrange the following numbers from largest to smallest: 50 55 45 85 99 69 100

   _____   [1]

43. The number 12 is divisible by which numbers? _____   [2]

_____

End of Mock Test. Please hand over the paper for assessment.

Mock Paper 3

Instructions

1. You have 35 minutes to answer the questions. Total marks 42

2. If you are unable to answer any questions, please move on to the next question

3. This is an advanced level 3 test

1. 35 divided by 7 is _____ [1

2. How many maximum 5p coins can you get if you have 15p? _____ [1

3. How many animals did you see if you saw 2 giraffes, 1 tiger, 5 crocodiles, and 2 pandas in the zoo? _____ [1

4. If Zane's dad gave him 12 chocolates, how many chocolates can he and his 3 friends have so that all of them get an equal number to share? _____ [1

5. Izi has the above amount of money in the bag.

(a) How much money does Izi have? _____

(b) With the above money, Izi buys a sticker book that costs 90 pence. How much money is still left with Izi? _____

(c) After buying the sticker, Izi can now buy a big ice cream for £2.90 or a cake for £2.85. What should Izi buy if she wants to have the least money left with her? _____

(d) If Izi decides to buy the ice cream for £2.90 in the end, draw the change left with Izi.

[4

6. Map the circled numbers to the number line. As an example, one of the circled numbers has already been mapped to the number line.

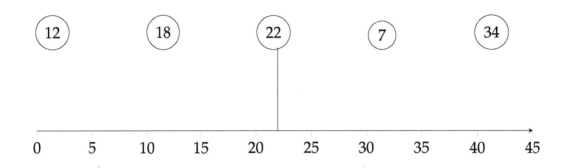

[2.

7. Francisco had 31 marbles. These were shared equally between Francisco and 6 friends. Each child got _____ marbles. There were _____ marbles left over.

[

8. Half of 22 is _____

[

9. How many maximum 2p coins can make 20p _____

[

10. If you invite 12 friends to the party, but 3 don't turn up, how many friends did you have at the party? _____

[

11. If you run 480 meters, how many kilometres have you run? _____

[

12. Xavier catches 5 fish, Andrea 4 fishes and Rumi 7 fishes; how many fish have been caught? _____ [1]

Solve questions 13-24

13.
$$\begin{array}{r} 29 \\ + 36 \\ \hline \end{array}$$
[1]

16.
$$\begin{array}{r} 445 \\ - 264 \\ \hline \end{array}$$
[1]

14.
$$\begin{array}{r} 245 \\ + 109 \\ \hline \end{array}$$
[1]

17.
$$\begin{array}{r} 201 \\ + 398 \\ \hline \end{array}$$
[1]

15.
$$\begin{array}{r} 456 \\ - 380 \\ \hline \end{array}$$
[1]

18. Which is bigger $\frac{1}{12}$ or $\frac{1}{13}$? _____ [2]

19. Which is smaller $\frac{10}{15}$ or $\frac{5}{15}$? _____ [2]

20. $45 + 38 =$ _____ [1]

21. 37 + 123 = _____ [1

22. 10 + 40 + 20 = _____ [1

23. 50 + 60 + 34 = _____ [1

24. 80 - 35 = _____ [1

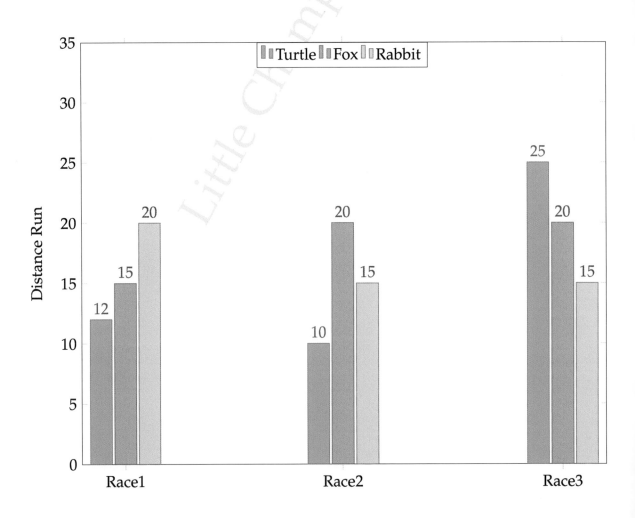

Answer questions 25-29 based on the above

25. Who won Race 1? _____ [1]

26. The Fox won race 2 by twice the distance run by the Turtle? (True/False) _____ [1]

27. Who ran the most distance if you add up all the races? _____ [1]

28. Who finished second in two races? _____ [1]

29. What is the maximum distance that anyone ran in a single race? _____ [1]

30. I travelled around a square measuring 5 cms. What is the total distance I travelled?

_____ [1.5]

31. Round 25 to the nearest ten _____ [1]

32. 5+4 = 4+5, True/False _____ [1]

Answer questions 33-35 based on the below

Jamie is 100 cm tall, Lizzie is 5 cm taller than Jamie and Shiv is 10 cm shorter than Jamie

33. Who is the tallest? _____ [

34. What is the difference in height between Lizzie and Shiv _____ [

35. What is the total of the heights of the three children? _____ [

_____

End of Mock Test. Please hand over the paper for assessment.

Mock Paper 4

Instructions

1. You have 35 minutes to answer the questions. Total marks 58

2. If you are unable to answer any questions, please move on to the next question

3. This is an advanced level 4 test

1. What is the total of the above dominos?   _____   [1]

2. What is the total of the above dominos?   _____   [1]

3. What is the total of the above dominos?   _____   [1]

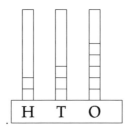

H   T   O

For the above abacus, please answer questions 4-6

4. What is the number shown in the abacus? _____   [1

5. If we remove one bead from Ten's and add it to One's, what is the new number
   that will be visible on the abacus? _____   [1

6. What is the biggest number you can form by moving all of the One's beads to
   Hundred's? _____   [1

7. Dona has 40 marbles rounded to the nearest ten, Gabriel has 60 marbles rounded
   to the nearest ten, and Katza has 20 marbles rounded to the nearest ten.

   (a) What is the difference between the minimum and maximum marbles that the
       group has? _____

   (b) What is the difference between the maximum of Gabriel and Katza's marbles?
       _____

[4]

8. Dorion started the race at 11:20 am and finished it a 1:07 pm, Lizzie started the race at 10:27 am and finished at 12:23 pm, and Andy started the race at 11:13 am and finished at 1:47 pm

   (a) Who finished fastest? _____

   (b) If Andy wanted to finish in the time that Dorion took to run, when should he have started to run if the end time remains the same? _____

[4]

9. I have five buses ready to transport children to a picnic?

   (a) Each bus needs to have at least 2 teachers. How many children can I take to the picnic if each bus can have a maximum of 20 people, including the driver?
   _____

   (b) If 25 children decide to come own their own to the picnic, how many buses are now needed ?
   _____

[3]

10. I divide a number by half and then subtract five. I am left with 55. What number did I start with? _____ [1.5]

11. A non-zero number divided by itself will equal 1. (True/False)
   _____ [2]

12. A non-zero number multiplied by 1 will give the same number as you started with (True/False) _____ [2

Solve questions 13-17 by showing calculations.

```
        15
13.   X 11
```
[1]

```
       689
16.  + 325
```
[1]

```
        9
14.   X 13
```
[1]

```
       570
17.  - 534
```
[1]

```
      312
15.  - 133
```
[1]

18. Ron can buy spend money on the above things. A car costs £2.50, plane £2.90, a box of chocolate £2.40 and the dog £4.80   [6]

    (a) If he has £10 and decides to buy the car and the plane, will he have enough money to buy the dog? Yes/No   _____

    (b) Which is the most expensive item that he can buy?   _____

    (c) How much would it cost if Ron wanted to buy the car, plane and chocolate box?   _____

    (d) If Ron buys a car and dog toy, how much change will he get?   _____

19. 25 rounded off to the nearest ten = _____   [1]

20. 91 rounded off to the nearest ten = _____ [1

21. After rounding off, I get a number 70. What is the smallest number that I possibly had before rounding off? _____ [1

22. After rounding off, I get a number 60. What is the largest number that I possibly had before rounding off? _____ [1

23. Write the time in words

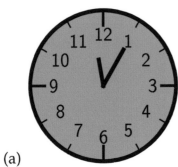

(a) _____

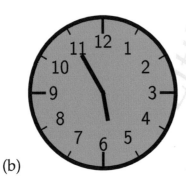

(b) _____

(c) 18:15 _____

(d) 11:50 am _____

[4]

24. Match the following by drawing connecting lines. Use your judgements of the weight of the following items

TV	4000g
Laptop	40kg
Microwave	1kg
Fridge	80kg
Kettle	10kg

[2.5]

Fill in the right operator (+, -, ÷, x) or the number as required.

25. $1.5km =$ ☐ $meters$ [1]

26. $12 \ X$ ☐ $= 180$ [1]

27. $65 \ + \ 35 \ -$ ☐ $= 72$ [1]

28. $29 +$ ☐ $= 69$ [1]

29. Answer the below questions about the chart. The chart has various age groups and the number of holidays they have taken in the past year.

(a) Which age group has been on the maximum number of holidays? _____

(b) How many holidays has the age group 0-2 taken? _____

(c) Age group 10-20 has taken 10 more holidays than age group 20-50. True/False?

_____

(d) If the number of holidays by 2-5 years is increased 3 times, the number of holidays will be more than the holidays of 50+ (True/False) _____

[4

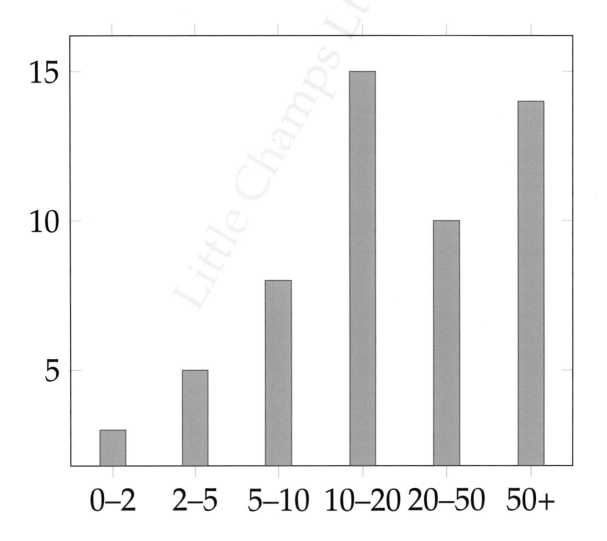

30. If 4 oranges cost 1.25, how much will 8 oranges cost? _____ [1]

31. If I walk 300 meters to a shop, I then walk another 1300 centimetres to the park and finally I walk 1 km to the school, how many kilometres have I walked?

    _____ [2]

32. Jack buys five oranges for £2.50; how much does each orange cost? [1]

33. I am twice the age of my cousin. My cousin's age is two multiplied by my sister's age. My sister is 6 years old. What is my age? _____ [2]

_____

End of Mock Test. Please hand over the paper for assessment.

Mock Paper 5

Instructions

1. You have 35 minutes to answer the questions. Total marks 56

2. If you are unable to answer any questions, please move on to the next question

3. This is an advanced level 5 test

Solve the following

1. $\frac{1}{4} = \frac{2}{8}$ True or False?   _____   [1

2. Three fourth of 12 =   _____   [1

3. $\frac{1}{4} + \frac{2}{4} + \frac{1}{4} = \frac{1}{4}$ True or False?   _____   [1

4. $\frac{1}{6} + \frac{5}{6} + \frac{8}{6} =$ _____   [1

5. I run around a rectangle where one side measures 8 cm and another measure 10 cm. What is the distance I have run?

   _____   [2

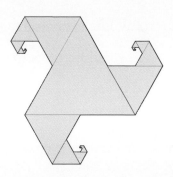

6. How many triangles can you see in the above image? _____ [2]

7. How many rectangles can you see in the above image? _____ [2]

Solve the following

8. $300 \div 10 =$ _____ [1]

9. $2500 \div 10 =$ _____ [1]

10. $30 \div 1 =$ _____ [1]

11. $12 \times 9 =$ _____ $\times 2$ [1]

12. $7 \times 8 =$ _____ $\times 4$ [1]

13. Use a ruler to measure the below line. The line measures _____ cm.   [1

Use the numbers 2, 5 and 3 to answer the below questions

14.   _____ x _____ = 10   [1

15.   _____ x 5 = 15   [1

16. 15 ÷ _____ = _____   [1

17.   _____ + _____ = 10 - _____   [1

18. Circle the odd numbers.

   20   14   18   29   19   26   33   45   28   [1

19. Circle the even numbers.

   49   50   26   33   53   79   86   40   55   85   100   [1

20. A pair of socks cost £3, five trousers cost £25. Raul has £40 and Seema has £55.

(a) How many trousers can Raul buy if he needs to buy at least 3 pair of socks?

_____

(b) Seema can buy twice the number of trousers compared to Raul, True/False?

_____

[2]

21. What will be the digital time if 2:30 (hr:min) is added to the time shown below?   [1]

22. Organise the following from largest to smallest

(a) 5 kg, 4.5 g, 45 g, 0.6 kg, 500 g, 5100g   _____

(b) 1 cm, 1 m, 1 mm, 4 cm, 45mm, 0.4 m, 1 km   _____

[2]

23. I divide a number by half and then multiply by 5. I am left with 25. What number did I start off with?   _____   [2]

24. Norma loves reading books. She has 20 books in the library and has read 12. She has now been gifted another 2. How many books are unread?. _____

[1

25. Ten multipled by 15 is _____

[1

26. I left home at 8:30 am for a class. I reached my friend's house after a 15-minute walk. I waited 5 minutes for my friend before we walked 10 minutes to get to the class. The class lasted for an hour. We then left and walked 10 minutes to the ice cream shop. We bought ice cream, and I walked 15 minutes to get to my home.

  (a) At what time did I reach home? _____

  (b) If I walked 10 minutes faster to my friend's place and spent 15 minutes less in the class, what time would I get back home? _____

[4

27. 2 mangoes cost £2, and 5 oranges cost £1.2. How much would 8 mangoes and 10 oranges cost? _____

[2

    Please answer 28-30 based on the below figure

28. What is the length of the number line in cm? _____

[1

29. Show 12 on the number line

[1

30. Show 22.5 on the number line   [1]

Number line...

0   5   10   15   20   25   30

31. Each row, column and diaognal add up to the same total of 34. Can you find the
    missing number in the empty squares?   [4]

	2	16	
	13		6
1	8		15
14		5	

32. Fill in the right operator (+, -, ÷, x) or the number as required.

(a) $365 - \boxed{} = 355$

(b) $20 + 10 + 30 - \boxed{} = 45$

(c) $10X \boxed{} = 100$

(d) $18 + 19 + \boxed{} = 77$

[4

33. Draw a mirror image of the below pattern [2

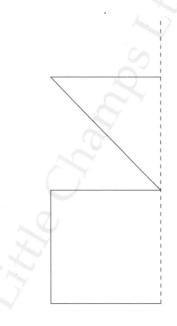

Use the correct operator ($<$, $>$, $=$) to fill in the boxes

34. 85 $\boxed{}$ 85 [1

35. 36 $\boxed{}$ 46 [1

36. 13 $\boxed{}$ 31 [1

Votes received by Food Items

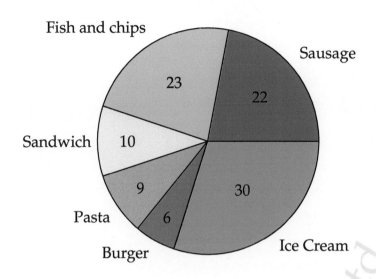

37. In the above pie-chart, which is the most popular food item? [1]

38. What is the total number of votes received across all food items? [1]

39. How many more votes do Fish and Chips need to become most popular food item? [1]

End of Mock Test. Please hand over the paper for assessment.

MOCK PAPER 1

Solve the following

1. 40	3. 45	5. 95	7. 0
2. 39	4. 5	6. 90	8. 20

Answer whether each statement is True or False

9. True

10. False

11. False

12. True

13. 189, 190, 198, 232, 323, 423

14. 463, 435, 243, 143, 43

15. See below   (a) 21   (c) 1

                   (b) 3   (d) 5

Write the following numbers as words

16. Forty three

17. One hundred and twenty five

18. Ten

19. Nineteen

20. Twenty eight

21. see below

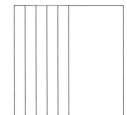

22. see below

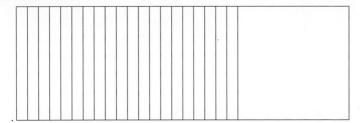

23. see below

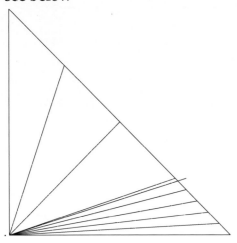

24. 8   25. 31   26. 16   27. 13   28. 45 minutes

29. see below

   (a) Park

   (b) True

30. £18

31. 15 km

32. Four hundred and fifty

33. One hundred and forty

34. Eight hundred and forty three

35. Seven hundred and eighty four

36. Top left: 7 Top right: 2 Bottom left: 1 Bottom right: 2

37. See below

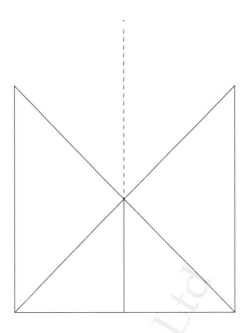

38. >   39. <   40. <   41. <   42. =   43. 20

44. quarter past ten in the morning or something similar

45. eleven o'clock

MOCK PAPER 2

1. (a) Zoe   (b) $\frac{1}{3}$ (c) False

2. 36   3. 10   4. $\frac{1}{9}, \frac{1}{12}$ 5. 9, 11   6. 10, 50

7. 46   8. 108   9. 100   10. 12   11. 6

12. 1

13. (a) 1:30 pm   (b) 6 hours 30 minutes   (c) 11:45 am

14. Sixty seven

15. Four hundred and eighty five

16. Thirty five

17. Fifty nine

18. See below

19. Square

20. Triangle

21. Pentagon

22. Circle

23. Hexagon

24. 7

25. 106

26. X

27. ÷

28. 20

29. 59

30. Quarter past twelve or something similar

31. Quarter to seven or something similar

32. Thirty six minutes past three pm

33. Nine forty am

34. 6   35. 50   36. 800   37. 100   38. 61   39. 8:35 am

40. (a) 12

    (b) 12, 21, 30

41. 19, 23, 24, 32, 34, 56, 235

42. 100, 99, 85, 69, 55, 50, 45

43. 1, 2, 3, 4, 6, 12 (at least two numbers are expected)

MOCK PAPER 3

1. 5   2. 3   3. 10   4. 4

5.   (a) £3.83 or three pounds eighty three pence

     (b) £2.93 or two pounds ninety three pence

     (c) ice cream

     (d) 3p left. drawing of 1 and 2 pence coin expected

6. see below

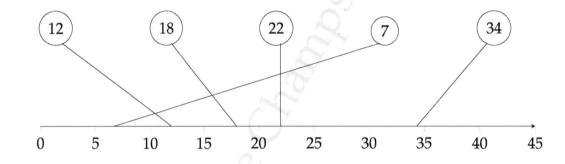

7. 4, 3	12. 16	17. 599	22. 70	27. fox	32. True
8. 11	13. 65	18. $\frac{1}{12}$	23. 144	28. fox	33. Lizzie
9. 10	14. 354	19. $\frac{5}{15}$	24. 45	29. 25	
10. 9	15. 76	20. 83	25. rabbit	30. 20 cms	34. 15 cm
11. .48 km	16. 181	21. 160	26. true	31. 30	35. 295 cm

MOCK PAPER 4

1. 10   2. 12   3. 16   4. 235   5. 226   6. 730

7. (a) 44   (b) 40

8. (a) Dorion   (b) 12 pm

9. (a) 85   (b) 4

10. 120   12. true   14. 117   16. 1,014

11. true   13. 165   15. 179   17. 36

18. (a) no   (c) £7.8

     (b) dog   (d) £2.7

19. 30   20. 90   21. 65   22. 59

23. any answer similar to below is acceptable

     (a) five past eleven

     (b) five to six

     (c) quarter past six in the evening

     (d) ten to noon

24. TV - 40 kg, Laptop - 1 kg, Microwave - 10 kg, Fridge - 80 kg, Kettle - 400g

25. 1500   26. 15   27. 28   28. 40

29. (a) 10-20   (c) quarter past six in the evening

     (b) 2   (d) ten to noon

30. £2.50   31. 1.313   32. 50p   33. 24

MOCK PAPER 5

1. True   3. False   5. 36 cm

2. 9   4. 14/6 or 7/3   6. 11

7. 8. (Anything above 5 is acceptable)

8. 30   10. 30   12. 14   14. 2,5   16. 5,3

9. 250   11. 54   13. 6.4 cm   15. 3   17. 5,3,2

18. 29, 19, 33, 45   19. 50, 26, 86, 40, 100

20. (a) 1   (b) True

21. 13:30

22. (a) 5100g, 5kg, 0.6kg, 500g, 45g, 4.5g   (b) 1km, 1m, 0.4m, 45mm, 4cm, 1cm, 1mm

23. 10   24. 10   25. 150

26. (a) 10:25 am   (b) 10 am

27. £10.4   28. 12.7 cm   29. see below   30. see below

0	5	10	15	20	25	30

12   22.5

31. see below

7	2	16	9
12	13	3	6
1	8	10	15
14	11	5	4

32. (a) 10   (b) 15   (c) 10   (d) 40

33. see below

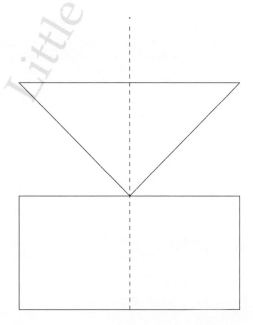

34. =   35. <   36. <   37. ice cream 38. 100   39. 8

Printed in Great Britain
by Amazon

17185311R00029